Gracious Elegance

The pineapple-classic symbol of hospitality-inspires these three timeless designs.

(1) Size: 29cm in diameter. Instructions on page 67

1

3

(2) Size: 33 cm in diameter. Instructions on page 68

(3) Size: 25 cm in diameter. Instructions on page 69

Delicate Duo

You'll be delighted with the cool beauty of these accent pieces.

(4) Size: 34cm in diameter. Instructions on page 70

(5) Size: 39cm in diameter. Instructions on page 71

Light and Lively

Cord is the novel, handsome reason these designs are so successful.

(6) Size: 28cm in diameter. Instructions on page 72

(7) Size: 28cm in diameter. Instructions on page 73

Altogether Lovely

A marvelous focal point for any room in your home.

(8) Size: 31cm in diameter. Instructions on page 74

Before you begin...

★ Relationship between thread and hook

In order to have your crocheting turn out beautifully, choose a hook that is the correct size for the yarn. In this book, only thick cotton threads are used, requiring a 1.75 mm-1.50 mm size hook. The commonly used cotton thread requires a 1.00 mm-0.90 mm size hook.

★ How to hold the hook and yarn

With the left hand, hold the end of the yarn over your fingers as shown. Hold the crochet hook in your right hand.

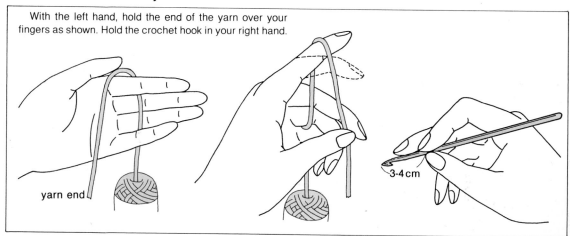

yarn end

3-4 cm

★ How to start

Make a chain (ch) of the required number of stitches (st).
1. Turn the hook as indicated by the arrow.
2. Draw the yarn through and pull down on the yarn end to tighten.
3. Make a chain.
4. 1 chain stitch completed.
5. Continue drawing yarn through each loop in this manner.

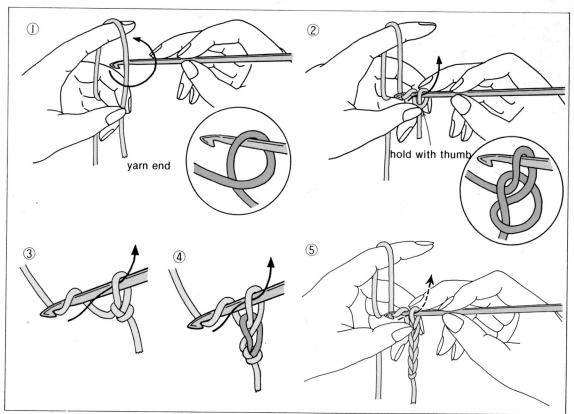

① yarn end

② hold with thumb

③

④

⑤

To begin a circle

★ **Form a ring with ch sts, then single crochet (sc) (example: sample 7)**

1. Wind the yarn around your index finger twice loosely and draw it through the ring thus formed.
2. Yarn over hook: draw yarn through loop on hook.
3. Single crochet (sc)
4. Required number of sc (6sc) completed.
5. Pull yarn end to tighten.
6. Sl st to first st, and continue to Row 2.

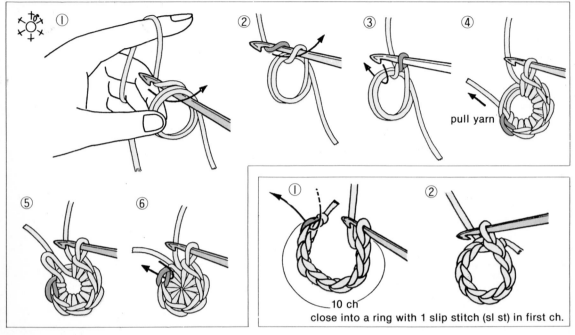

pull yarn

10 ch
close into a ring with 1 slip stitch (sl st) in first ch.

★ **Form a ring with double crochet (dc) (example: sample 11)**

1. Wind yarn around your index finger twice loosely, close with 1 sc in ring.
2. Start with 3 ch, then crochet required number of dc.
3. With sl st get to first loop of 3 ch.
4. Start Row 2 with 3 ch.
5. Continue with dc.

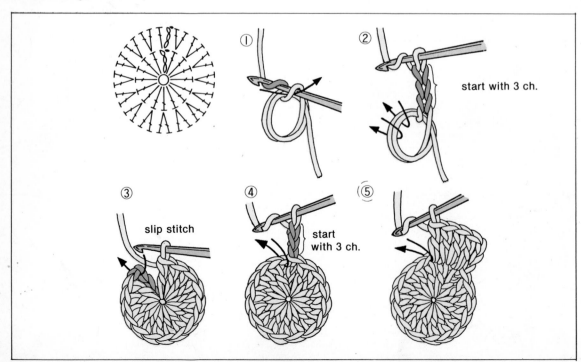

start with 3 ch.

slip stitch

start with 3 ch.

★ How to start the first row (sc)

1. Insert hook in the back of second chain from hook, yarn over hook, draw yarn through loop.
2. Yarn over hook, draw yarn through 2 loops on hook.
3. 1 sc completed. Crochet the next sc as indicated by the arrow.
4. Row 1 completed.

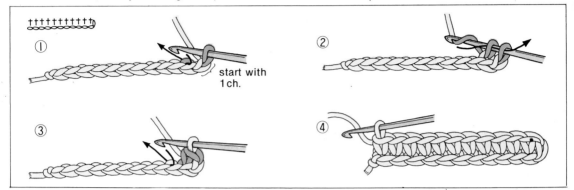

★ How to start the first row (dc)

1. Start with 3 ch, yarn over hook.
2. Insert hook in stitch, yarn over hook, draw yarn through stitch.
3. Draw yarn through 2 loops as indicated.
4. Draw yarn through 2 loops again.
5. Crochet the next dc as indicated.

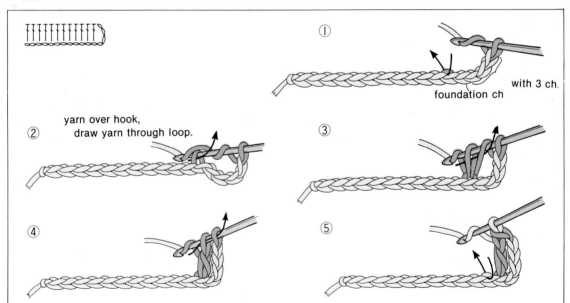

★ Chain stitches and the length of other stitches

To begin, make a chain of the required number of ch sts. First row: start with the number of ch sts that make a length equal to the stitch you are using. The first ch st in sc is not counted as a sc, but the others are.

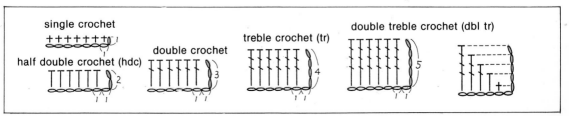

single crochet

half double crochet (hdc)

double crochet

treble crochet (tr)

double treble crochet (dbl tr)

Basic stitches and symbols

International symbols for stitches are used in this book
(see bottom of p13). In addition, a plus sign (+) is
used to indicate in which stitch a sc is to be made.

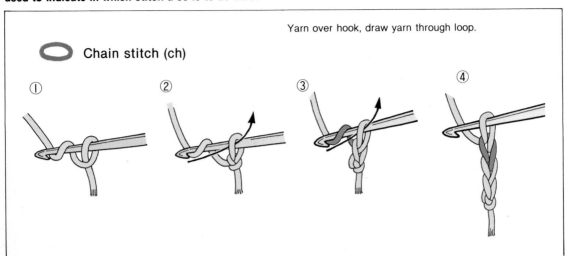

Yarn over hook, draw yarn through loop.

Chain stitch (ch)

① ② ③ ④

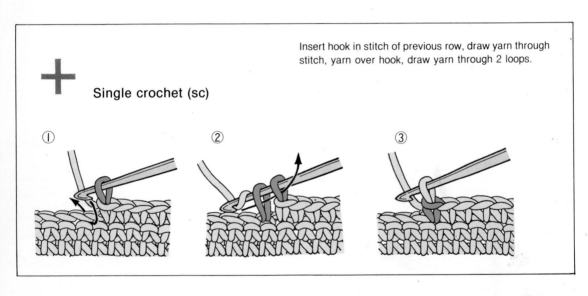

Insert hook in stitch of previous row, draw yarn through
stitch, yarn over hook, draw yarn through 2 loops.

Single crochet (sc)

① ② ③

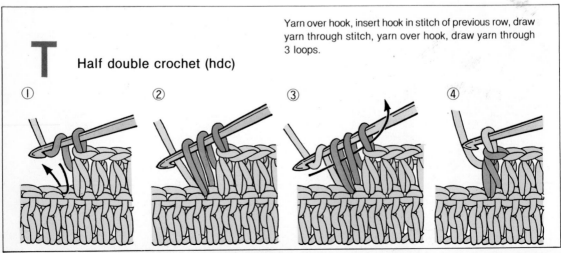

Yarn over hook, insert hook in stitch of previous row, draw
yarn through stitch, yarn over hook, draw yarn through
3 loops.

Half double crochet (hdc)

① ② ③ ④

Double crochet (dc)

Make 3 loops as in hdc, yarn over hook, draw yarn through 2 loops, yarn over hook, draw yarn through 2 remaining loops.

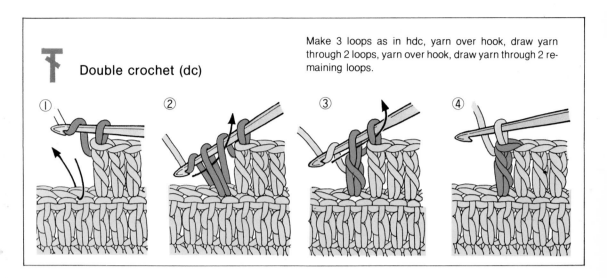

Treble crochet (tr)

Yarn over hook twice, draw yarn through stitch of previous row making 4 loops as in dc, yarn over hook, draw yarn through 2 loops at once 3 times.

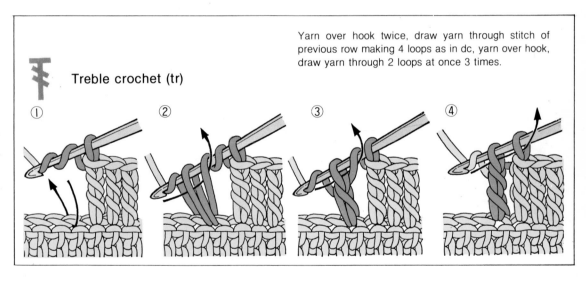

Slip stitch (sl st)

Insert hook in stitch of previous row, yarn over hook, draw yarn through stitch and the loop on hook together.

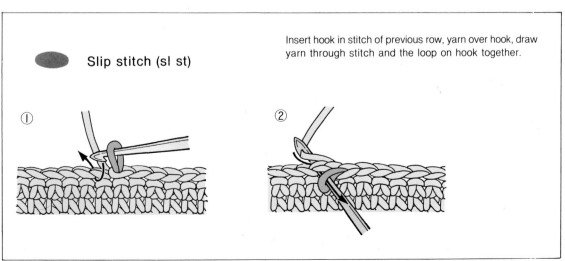

Puff stitch (3 dc)

Work 3 half-closed dc on same stitch of previous row, complete by drawing yarn through all half-closed dc at once.

 ① 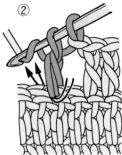 ② 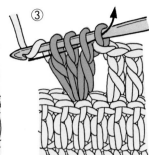 ③  ④

Cluster (2 sc)

Work 2 half-closed sc in previous row, yarn over hook, draw yarn through all loops on hook at once.

① 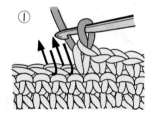 ② 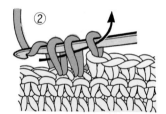 ③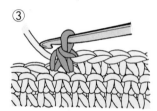

Cluster (2 dc)

Work 2 half-closed dc in previous row, yarn over hook, draw yarn through all loops on hook at once.

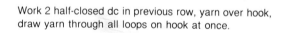

① ② ③ ④
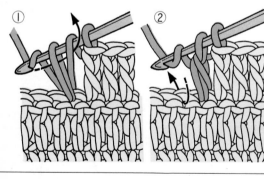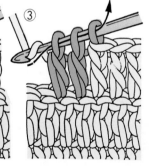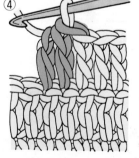

Picot (p)

① Chain 3   ②   ③
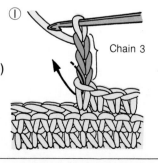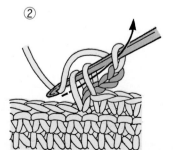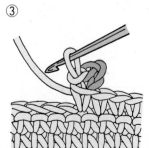

To increase (sc)

Work 2 sc in same st of previous row.

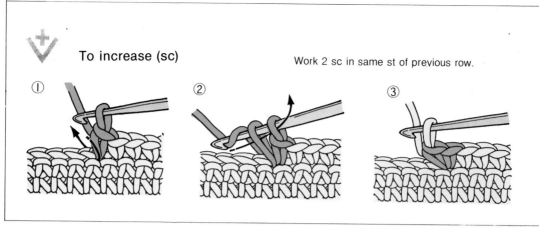

Cross stitch (dc)

Work 1 dc left of two stitches of previous row, work 1 dc in right stitch as shown with arrow, wrapping the first dc.

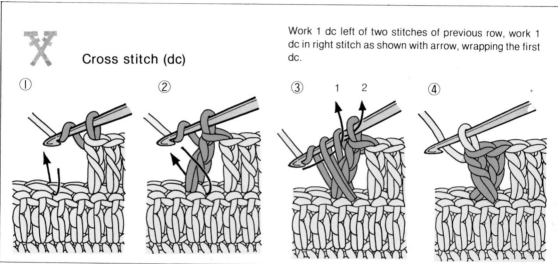

Popcorn stitch (5 dc)

Work 5 dc in same stitch of previous row, leave last loop on hold, insert hook from front of first dc, then sl st loop on hold. Yarn over hook, ch st.

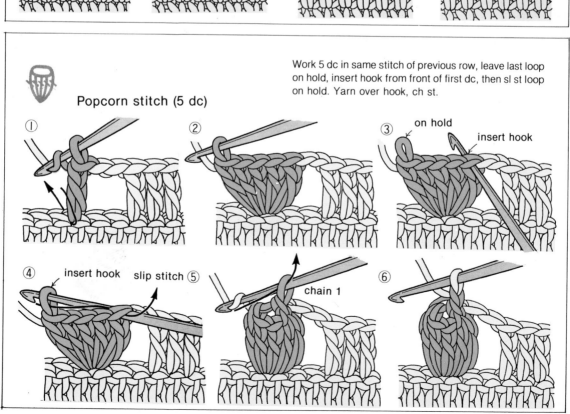

How to start the next row (example: net pattern)

★ With slip stitch
1. With slip stitch get to the first stitch.
2. Slip stitch (2 sts) to get to starting position of the next row.

★ With other stitches
1. Work fewer ch (2 sts), 1 dc in first stitch (1 dc = 3 ch).
2. Start row 2 from there.

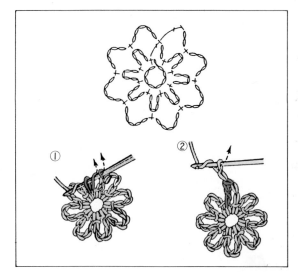

Finishing

★ Slip stitch
1. With slip stitch get to first loop starting chain.
2. Slip stitch as shown.
3. Work yarn through back edge and finish points.

★ Using a needle
1. Break off yarn, leaving an 8 cm end. Pull out loop on hook to get yarn end , insert needle in place, draw yarn through stitch.
2. Insert needle in last stitch from the top, draw through as shown.
3. Work yarn through 3-4 cm of back edge and break off.

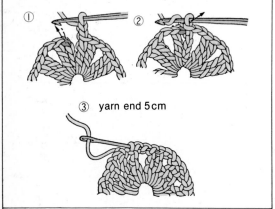

③ yarn end 5 cm

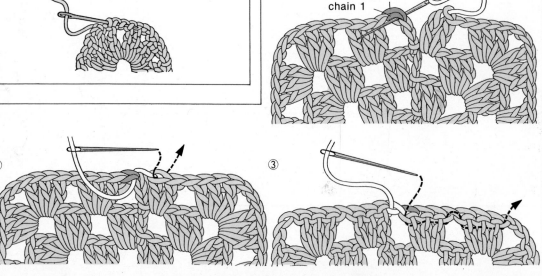

pick up 2

chain 1

Classic Serenity

Even hurried snacks are more refreshing when this is your table centerpiece.

Size: 31cm in diameter. Instructions on page 20

9

★**Materials:** Crochet cotton DMC (Soft twisted), 40 g white (BLANC) Crochet hook size 1.75 mm
★**Finished size:** 31 cm in diameter
★**Instructions:** Chain 9 and close into a ring. **Row 1:** start with 4 ch, 1 cluster (2 tr), °5 ch, 1 cluster (3 tr)°, repeat from ° to ° 7 times, 5 ch. close with sl st. **Row 2:** Work net pattern of 5 ch. **Row 3:** same as Row 1, increasing number of ch sts. **Rows 4—5:** work net pattern, being careful of number of ch sts. **Rows 6—7:** work 16 pattern sets as shown in design. **Rows 8—10:** work net pattern of 5 ch. **Rows 11—12:** same as Rows 6—7. **Rows 13—16:** work net pattern. **Rows 17 — 18:** work 16 scallop patterns. **Rows 19—21:** work net pattern by increasing 1 ch for each successive row.

★**Materials:** Crochet cotton DMC (Soft twisted) 35 g white (BLANC) outside flowers-25 g white (BLANC), 10 g peony rose (957) Crochet hook size 1.75 mm

★**Finished size:** 24 cm in diameter

★**Instructions:** White center: **Row 1**:chain 3 in ring, °4 ch, 1 dc°, repeat from °to °5 times, 4 ch, close with sl st. **Row**

2: work 6 petals, **Row 3:** pulling the previous row of petals toward you, sc on Row 1. **Row 4:** work 6 petals. **Row 5:** °5 ch. 1 sc°, repeat. **Row 6:** start with 3 ch, °5 ch, 1 dc°, repeat **Row 7:** work sc around. **Row 8—12:**increase 6 sts on Rows 9-11. **Row 13:** work sc around, decreasing 6 sts. Make the outside flowers, using pink yarn for the petals on Row 2.

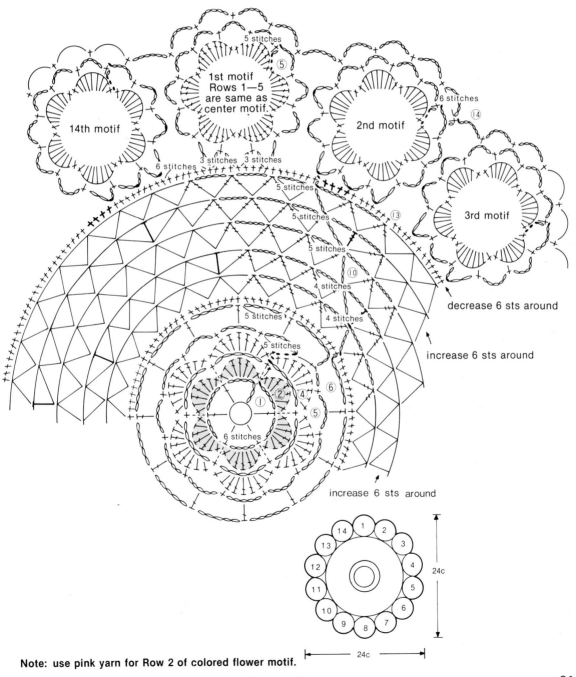

Note: use pink yarn for Row 2 of colored flower motif.

10

11

Spring Blossoms

These flowers last all year, blooming wherever
these lovely designs are to be found.

(10) Size: 24 cm in diameter. Instructions on page 21

(11) Size: 27 cm in diameter. Instructions on page 24

11

★**Materials:** Crochet cotton DMC (Soft twisted), 40 g white (BLANC) Crochet hook size 1.50 mm

★**Finished size:** 27 cm in diameter

★**Instructions: Row 1:** start with 3 ch in ring, 15 dc. **Row 2:** 3 ch, popcorn (4 dc), °3 ch, popcorn (5 dc)°, repeat from ° to ° 7 times, 3 ch, close with sl st. **Row 3:** make 8 petals.

Row 4: °1 sc, 7 ch°, repeat. **Row 5:** 3 ch, °5 c, 1 dc°, repeat from ° to °. **Row 6:** 3 ch, dc around. **Rows 7—13:** start with 1 ch, °1sc, 5 ch, 1 p (3 ch)°, repeat from ° to °. **Row 14:** 3 ch, 1 dc, °5 ch, 3 dc°, repeat from ° to °. **Row 15:** °work 7 dc in loop of 5 ch of previous row, repeat. Attach 16 flowers to center motif.

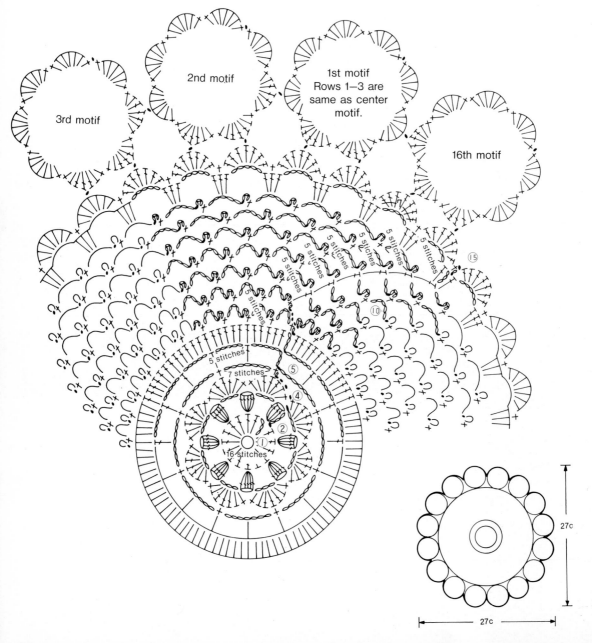

2nd motif

1st motif
Rows 1—3 are same as center motif.

3rd motif

16th motif

5 stitches

15

10

5 stitches
7 stitches
5
4
2
16 stitches
1

27c

27c

24

12 13

★**Materials:** Crochet cotton DMC (Soft twisted) Doily 12: 25 g white (BLANC), Doily 13: 50 g white (BLANC) Crochet hook size 1.75mm

★**Finished size:** Doily 12: 26 cm in diameter Doily 13: 39 cm in diameter

★**Instructions:** Doily 12: **Row 1:** start with 3 ch in ring, 1 dc, °5 ch, 2dc°, repeat from ° to °. **Row 2:** with sl st get

to loop of 5 ch of previous row, 3 ch, 2 dc, °5 dc, 3 dc, 5 ch, 3 dc°, repeat from ° to °. **Rows 3—5:** work net pattern. **Row 6:** work 8 sets of pattern. **Rows 7—12:** work net pattern, increasing number of ch sts. **Row 13:** work 16 pattern sets. Doily 13: work to Row 19, increasing the number of stitches.

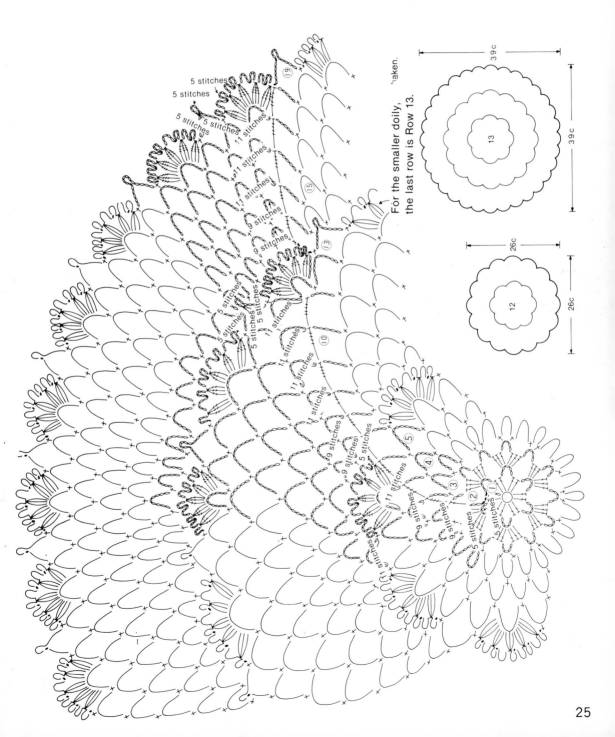

For the smaller doily, the last row is Row 13.

5 stitches
5 stitches
5 stitches
5 stitches
11 stitches
11 stitches
9 stitches
9 stitches
9 stitches
11 stitches
5 stitches
5 stitches
11 stitches
11 stitches
11 stitches
9 stitches
9 stitches
5 stitches
5 stitches
11 stitches
9 stitches

39 c
39 c
26 c
26 c

12

13

The Large and Small of It

Start with a doily. Then continue and make
a tablecloth, if you feel like it!

(12) Size: 26 cm in diameter. Instructions on page 25
(13) Size: 39 cm in diameter. Instructions on page 25

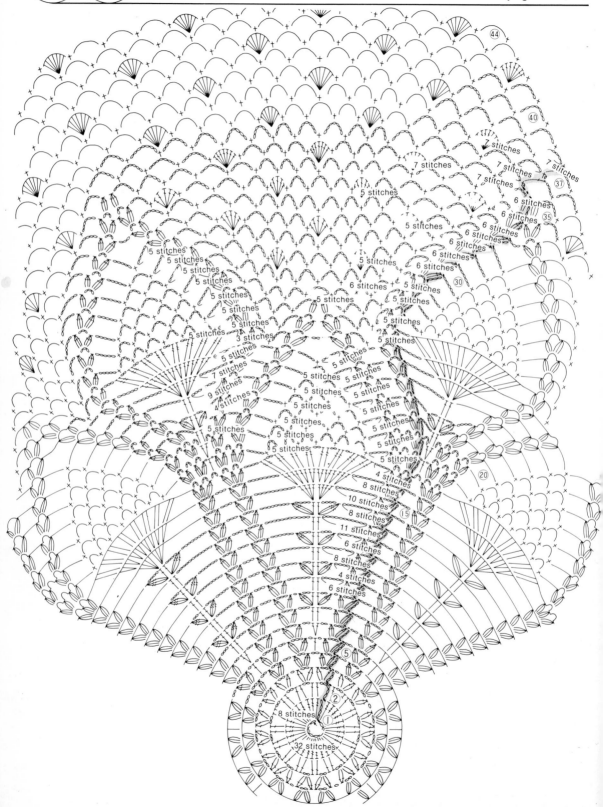

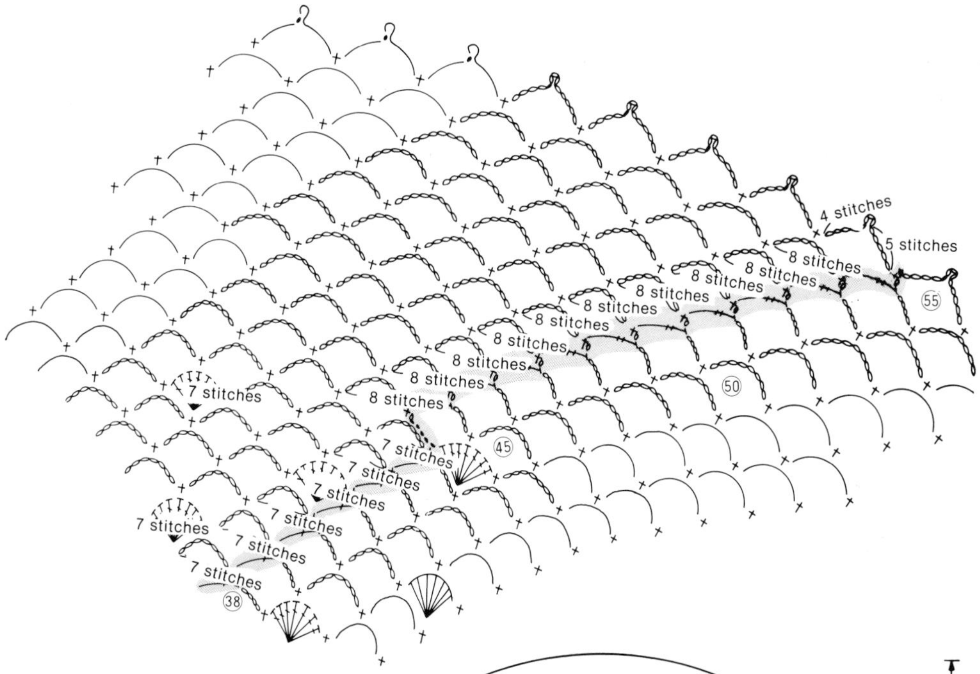

4 stitches
5 stitches
8 stitches
8 stitches
8 stitches
8 stitches
8 stitches
8 stitches
8 stitches
8 stitches
8 stitches
(55)
(50)
(45)
7 stitches
7 stitches
7 stitches
7 stitches
7 stitches
7 stitches
7 stitches
7 stitches
7 stitches
(38)

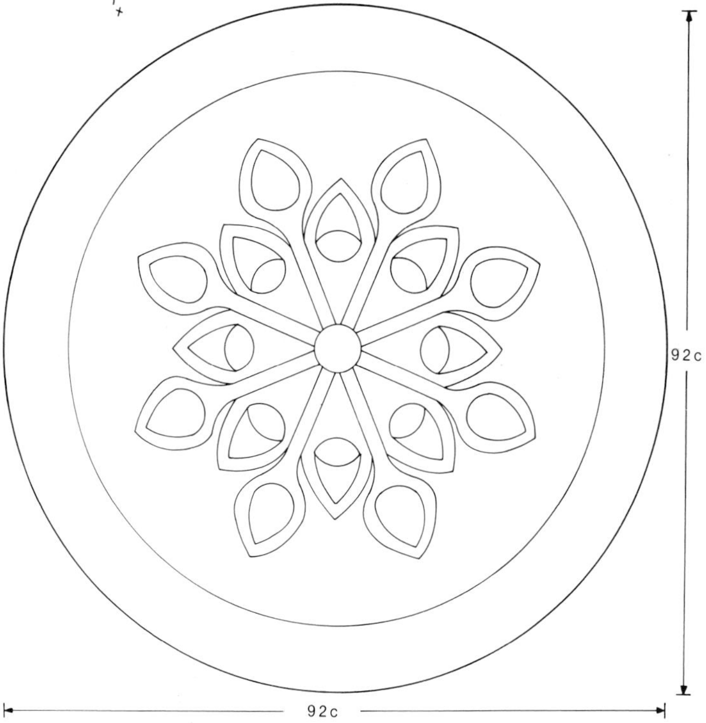

92c
92c

★**Materials:** Crochet cotton DMC (Soft twisted), Doily 14: 45 g, white (BLANC) Doily 15: 200 g, white (BLANC) Crochet hook size 1.75 mm

★**Finished size:** Doily 14: 33 cm in diameter. Doily 15: 92 cm in diameter

★**Instructions:** Doily 14: chain 8 and close into a ring. **Row 1:** start with 4 ch, 31 tr in ring. **Row 2:** start with 3 ch, °2ch, 2 dc°, repeat from ° to °. **Row 3:** 3 ch, 1 dc, repeat ch and cluster (2dc), being careful of number of sts. **Row 4:** add 2 ch between clusters (3dc). **Row 5:** work 8 foundations for pineapple pattern. **Rows 6—17:** continue work, being careful of number of sts between patterns. **Row 18:** work net pattern of 5 ch. **Row 19:** work p (4 ch) around edge. **Doily 15:** work pineapple patterns from Row 18 through 35. Work net and pine needle (5—7 dc in 1 st) patterns from Row 36 through 44. Work net pattern around from Row 45 through 55.

Continued on p. 75

14

15

(14) Size: 33 cm in diameter. Instructions on page 28

(15) Size: 92 cm in diameter. Instructions on page 28

★**Materials:** Crochet cotton DMC, 10 g white (BLANC)
Crochet hook size 1.75 mm
★**Finished size:** 16 cm in diameter
★**Instructions:** **Row 1:** start with 1 ch in ring, °1 sc, 3ch°, repeat. **Rows 2—5:** increasing the number of ch sts, work

net pattern. **Row 6:** 5 sc in each loop of 5 ch of previous row. **Row 7:** start with 1 ch, °1 sc, 1 p (3 ch), 6 ch°, repeat. **Row 8—14:** as in Row 7, work by increasing ch sts. **Row 15:** 1 ch, °°3 ch, °1 tr, 1 p (3 ch), 1 ch°, repeat from ° to ° 8 times, 2 ch, 1 sc°°, repeat from °° to °°

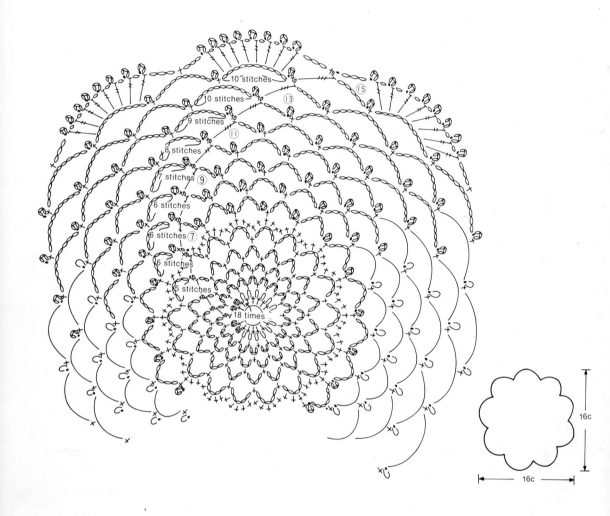

★**Materials:** Crochet cotton DMC, 10 g saffron (727)
Crochet hook size 1.75 mm
★**Finished size:** 17 cm in diameter
★**Instructions:** Chain 5 and close into a ring. **Row 1:** start

with 3 ch, °1 ch, 1dc°, repeat. **Row 2:** 3 ch, 1 cluster (2 dc), °3 ch, 1 cluster (3 dc)°, repeat from ° to °. **Row 3:** 1 ch, 40 sc. **Row 4:** 3 ch, °2 ch, 1 dc°, repeat from ° to °. **Row 5:** 1 ch, 60 sc. **Row 6—12:** make foundations for 20 pattern sets. **Row 13:** work 20 scallop patterns.

19

★**Materials:** Crochet cotton DMC, 10 g plum (52) Crochet hook size 1.75 mm
★**Finished size:** 18 cm in diameter
★**Instructions:** Chain 8 and close into a ring. **Row 1:** start with 1 ch, 16 sc, sl st to close. **Row 2:** start with 3 ch, °1 ch, 1 dc°, repeat. **Row 3** start with 3 ch, 4 dc, °1 ch, 5 dc°, repeat from ° to °. **Rows 4—7:** complete 8 pattern sets. **Row 8:** start with 1 ch, °1 sc, 1 p (3 ch), 6 ch°, repeat. **Rows 9—12:** same as Row 8, except add picots to Row 12.

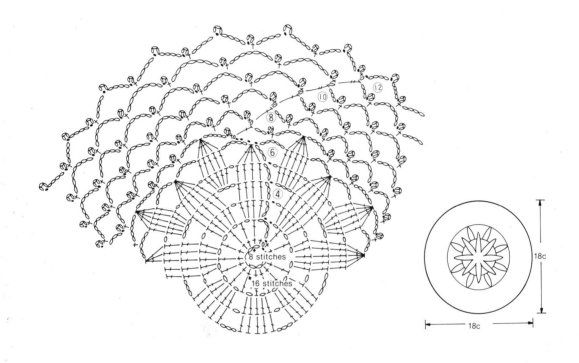

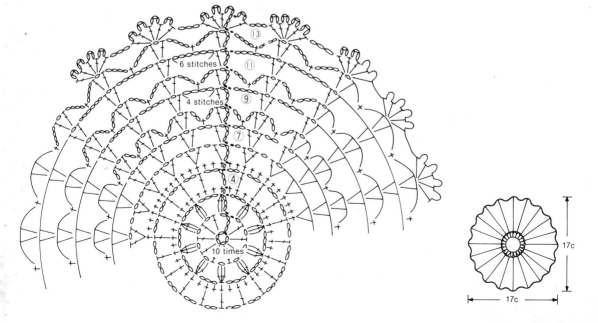

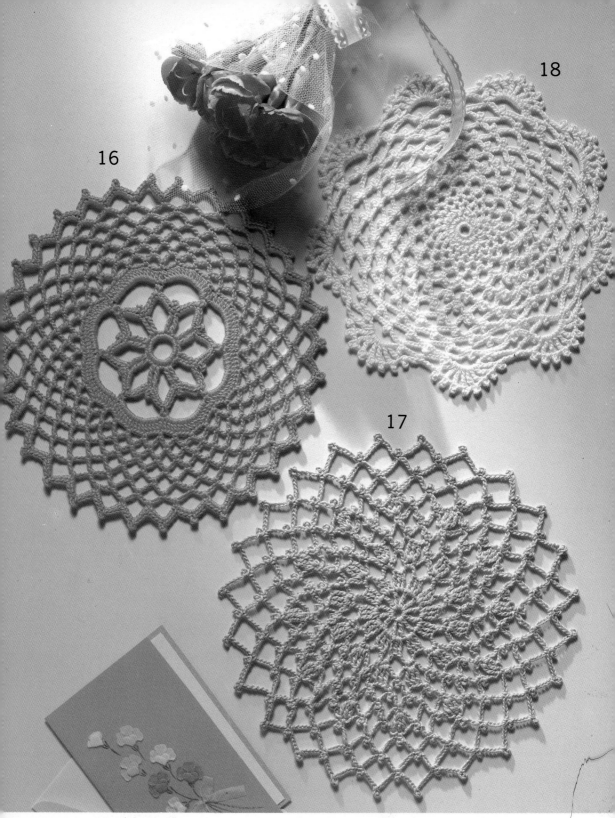

Minor Delights

That give maximum pleasure. Each is made from a 10-gram ball of cotton.

(16) Size: 17 cm in diameter. Instructions on page 36

(17) Size: 18 cm in diameter. Instructions on page 37

(18) Size: 16 cm in diameter. Instructions on page 32

(19) Size: 18 cm in diameter. Instructions on page 33
(20) Size: 17 cm in diameter. Instruction on page 32
(21) Size: 15.5 cm in diameter. Instructions on page 37

19

20

21

16

★**Materials:** Crochet cotton DMC, 10 g sky blue (518) Crochet hook size 1.75 mm

★**Finished size:** 17 cm in diameter

★**Instructions:** Chain 10 and close into a ring, **Row 1:** start with 1 ch, 24 sc, sl st to close. **Row 2:** start with 4 ch, 1 tr, ° 7 ch, 2 tr °, repeat from ° to °. **Row 3:** start with 1 ch, °° 1 sc, ° 1 p (3 ch), 5 sc °, repeat from ° to ° twice °°, repeat from °° to °°. **Row 4:** start with 1 ch, ° 1 sc, 10 ch, repeat. **Row 5:** work dc around. **Row 6—12:** work net pattern.

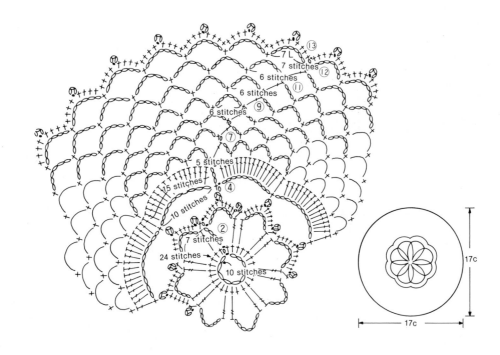

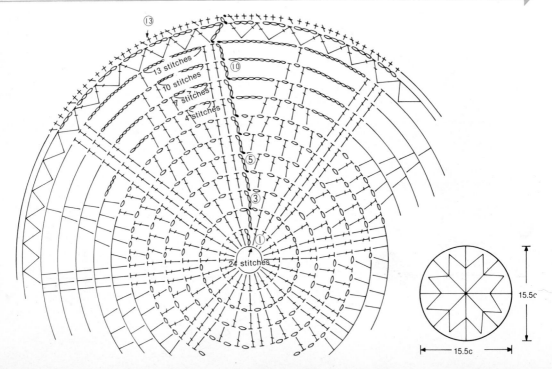

★**Materials:** Crochet cotton DMC, 10 g peony rose (957) Crochet hook size 1.75 mm
★**Finished size:** 18 cm in diameter
★**Instructions:** Chain 6 and close into a ring. **Row 1:** start with 4 ch, ° 2 ch, 1tr °, repeat. **Row 2:** start with 4 ch, 2 tr, ° 5 ch, 3 tr °, repeat from ° to °. **Row 3:** 3 ch, 1 sc, ° 7 ch, 1 sc, 3 ch, 1 sc °, repeat from ° to °. **Row 4:** °1 p (3 ch), 5 ch, 3 tr, 5 ch, 1 sc°, repeat. **Rows 5—10:** work ch, tr, and p around.

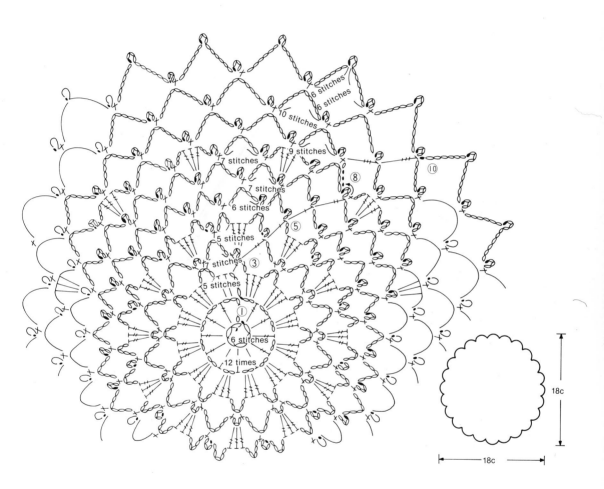

18c

18c

★**Materials:** Crochet cotton DMC, 10 g tangerine yellow (741) Crochet hook size 1.75 mm
★**Finished size:** 15.5 cm in diameter
★**Instructions:** **Row 1:** start with 3 ch in ring, 23 dc. **Row 2:** start with 3 ch, ° 1 ch, 1 dc°, repeat. **Row 3:** start with 3 ch, 2 dc, ° 1 ch, 1 dc, 1 ch, 3 dc °, repeat from ° to °. **Rows 4—11:** complete 8 of same pattern with dc and ch sts. **Row 12:** start with 3 ch, ° 3 ch, 1 cluster (2 dc)°, repeat. **Row 13:** work 4 sc in loop of 3 ch of previous row.

Concentrated Good Looks

A bumper crop of great designs, all made from one 50-gram ball of cotton.

(22) Size: 34 cm in diameter. Instructions on page 40

(23) Size: 22cm in diameter. Instructions on page 75

(24) Size: 23cm in diameter. Instructions on page 76

23

24

12 stitches
9 stitches
5 stitches
5 stitches
16 times
16 stitches
5 stitches
12 stitches
5 stitches
10 stitches
6 stitches
5 stitches
5 stitches
5 stitches
5 stitches
14 stitches
5 stitches
5 stitches
6 stitches
9 stitches
6 stitches
15 stitches
15 stitches
5 stitches
5 stitches
5 stitches
12 stitches
5 stitches
break off yarn
attach yarn
break off yarn
attach yarn

34c

34c

★**Materials:** Crochet cotton DMC (Soft twisted), 10 g sky blue (518), Crochet hook size 1.75 mm
★**Finished size:** 14 cm in diameter
★**Instructions:** Chain 7 and close into a ring. **Row 1:** start with 1 ch, 18 sc. **Row 2 :** start with 3 ch, 2 dc, ° 2 ch, 3 dc °, repeat from ° to ° **Row 3:** ° 5 ch, 5 sc °, repeat. **Row 4:** start with 3 ch, 7 dc, ° 3 ch, 8 dc °, repeat from ° to °. **Row 5—6:** start with 3 ch, 3 dc, ° 2 ch, 4 dc, 4 ch, 4 dc °, repeat from ° to °. **Row 7:** work sc and ch sts around. **Row 8:** start with 1 ch, complete 6 sets of pattern.

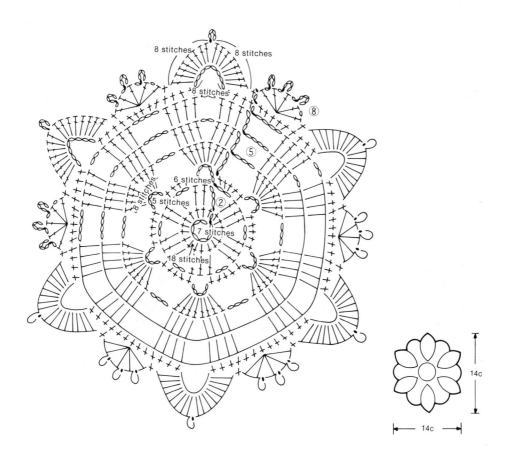

★**Materials:** Crochet cotton DMC (Soft twisted), 25 g white (BLANC) Crochet hook size 1.75 mm
★**Finished size:** 34 cm in diameter
★**Instructions: Row 1:** start with 3 ch in ring, 15 dc. **Row 2:** start with 3 ch ° 1 ch, 1 dc °, repeat. **Row 3:** 6 ch, ° 1 sc, 5 ch °, repeat from ° to °. **Row 4:** start with 4 ch, 1 cluster (2 tr), ° 5 ch, 1 cluster (3 tr)°, repeat from ° to °.

Rows 5—6: work net pattern, being careful of number of ch sts. **Row 7:** start with 4 ch, 2 tr, ° 5 ch 3 tr, 10 ch, 3 tr °, repeat from ° to °. **Row 8:** 4 ch, ° 3 tr, 5 ch, 3 tr, 3 ch, 1 sc, 3 ch °, repeat from ° to °. **Rows 9—10:** complete 16 sets of pattern. **Rows 11—16:** work a new pattern in 6 ch (beween each pattern) of previous row. For the last row, work p (3 ch) on top of each pattern.

(25) Size: 17cm in diameter. Instructions on page 44

(26) Size: 18cm × 18cm. Instructions on page 77

25

26

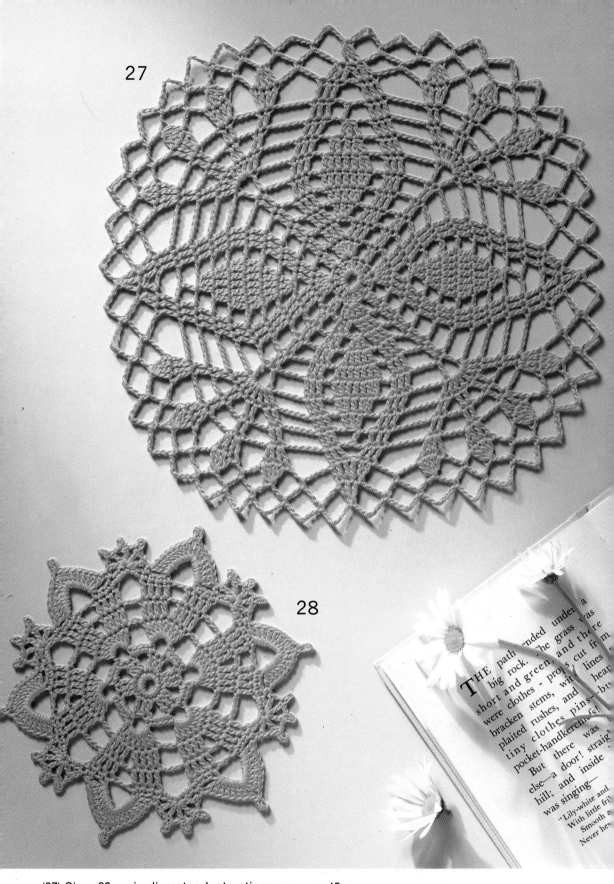

27

28

(27) Size: 22cm in diameter. Instructions on page 45
(28) Size: 14cm in diameter. Instructions on page 41

★**Materials:** Crochet cotton DMC (Soft twisted), 10 g sky blue (518) Crochet hook size 1.75 mm

★**Finished size:** 17 cm in diameter.

★**Instructions:** Chain 10 and close into a ring. **Row 1:** start with 3 ch, 23 dc in ring. **Row 2:** start with 3 ch, ° 5 ch, 1 dc °, repeat. **Row 3:** start with 3 ch, 2 dc, °5 ch, 3 dc °, repeat from ° to °. **Row 4:** start with 3 ch, 4 dc, ° 4 ch, 5 dc°, repeat from ° to °. **Rows 5—7:** work around being careful of number of ch and dc. **Row 8:** start with 3 ch, 4 dc, 1 cluster (2 dc),° 5 ch, 1 dc, 5 ch, 1 cluster (2 dc), 3 dc, 1 cluster (2 dc)°, repeat from ° to °. **Rows 9—10:** complete 8 sets of pattern at Row 9, work a new pattern between patterns at Row 10.

27

★**Materials:** Crochet cotton DMC (Soft twisted), 15 g sky blue (518), Crochet hook size 1.75 mm
★**Finished size:** 22 cm in diameter
★**Instructions:** Chain 6 and close into a ring. **Row 1:** start with 3 ch, 15 dc in ring. **Row 2:** start with 3 ch, 4 dc, ° 2 ch, 2 dc, 2 ch, 5 dc °, repeat from ° to °. **Row 3:** start with

3 ch, 2 dc, ° 3 ch, 3 dc, 2 ch, 2 dc, 2 ch 3 dc °, repeat from ° to °. **Rows 4—6:** work 4 sets of pattern. **Row 7:** start with 3 ch, 2 dc, ° 2 ch, 1 cluster (2 dc), 3 dc, 1 cluster (2 dc), 2 ch, 3 dc, 5 ch, 1 dc, 2 ch, 1 dc, 5 ch, 3 dc °, repeat from ° to °. **Rows 8—12:** work 4 sets of pattern. **Row 13:** start with 3 ch, work 1 cluster (2 dc) and net of 7 ch around.

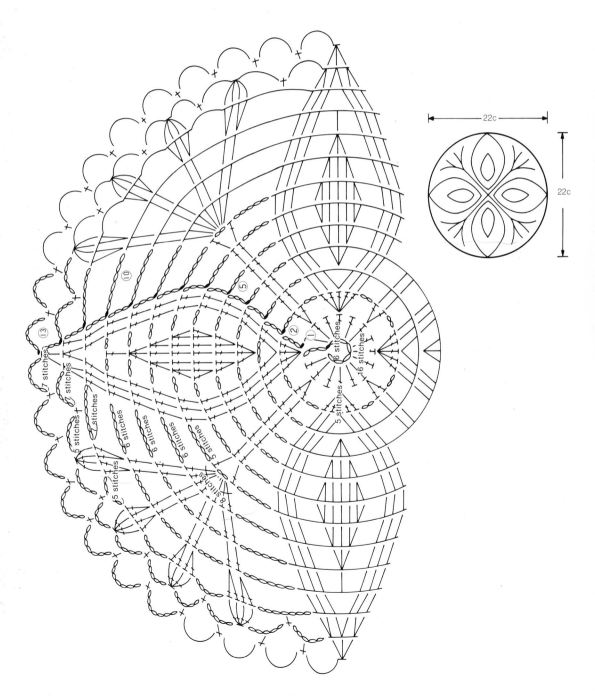

29

30

Custom Fit

Superb designs to shift and shape to suit your needs and space.

(29) Size: 45 cm × 31 cm. Instructions on page 48

(30) Size: 68 cm × 43 cm. Instructions on page 48

★Materials: Crochet cotton DMC (Soft twisted), Doily 29: 50 g white (BLANC). Doily 30: 115 g white (BLANC). Crochet hook 1.75 mm

★Finished size: Doily 29: 45 cm × 31 cm. Doily 30: 68 cm × 43 cm

★Instructions: Doily 29: **Row 1:** start with 3 ch in ring, ° 3 ch, 1 dc°, repeat. **Row 2:** start with 4 ch, 1 tr, ° 4 ch, 2 tr, 2 ch, 2 tr, 4 ch, 2 tr°, repeat from ° to °. **Row 3:** start with 4 ch, 1 tr, ° 5 ch, 3 tr, 3 ch, 3 tr, 5 ch, 2 tr °, repeat from ° to °. **Row 4:** start with 1 ch, ° sc, 8 ch, 1 sc, 6 ch, 4 tr, 6 ch, 4 tr, 6 ch ° 1 sc, repeat. **Row 5:** start with 1 ch, ° 15 sc, 6 ch, 5 tr, 6 ch, 1 sc, 6 ch, 5 tr, 6 ch °, repeat. **Row 6:** start with 4 ch, ° 4 ch, 1 dc, 4 ch, 1 tr, 6 ch, 1 cluster (5 tr), 6 ch, 1 sc, 6 ch, 1 sc, 6 ch, 1 tr°, repeat. **Row 7:** join from this row starting with 2nd motif. **Doily 30:** work 8 rows.

Doily 29 (Centerpiece)   **Small**

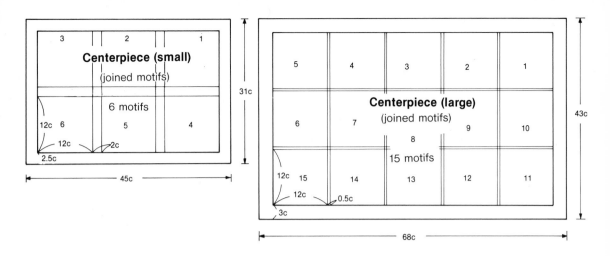

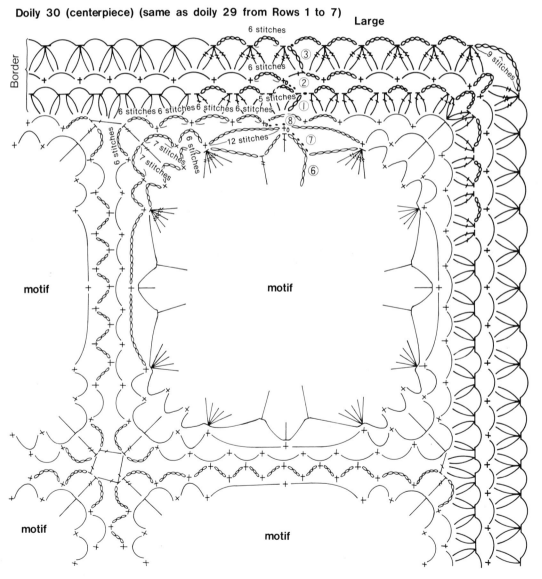

Doily 30 (centerpiece) (same as doily 29 from Rows 1 to 7)

49

31

32

(31) Size: 28 cm in diameter. Instructions on page 52

(32) Size: 74 cm in diameter. Instructions on page 77

★**Materials:** Crochet cotton DMC (Soft twisted) 20 g wihte (BLANC) Crochet hook size 1.75 mm

★**Finished size:** 28 cm in diameter

★**Instructions:** Chain 8 and close into a ring. **Row 1:** start with 3 ch, 23 dc in ring. **Row 2:** start with 3 ch, °3 ch, 1 dc°, repeat. **Row 3:** work 5 dc in loop of 3 ch of previous row. **Row 4:** °7 ch, 1 sc°, repeat. **Row 5:** start with 3 ch, 3 ch, 1 dc, °4 ch, 1 dc, 3 ch, 1 dc°, repeat from ° to °, making foundantion for patterns. **Rows 6—12:** work 6 sets of pineapple patterns. **Rows 13—15:** work net pattern with picots around.

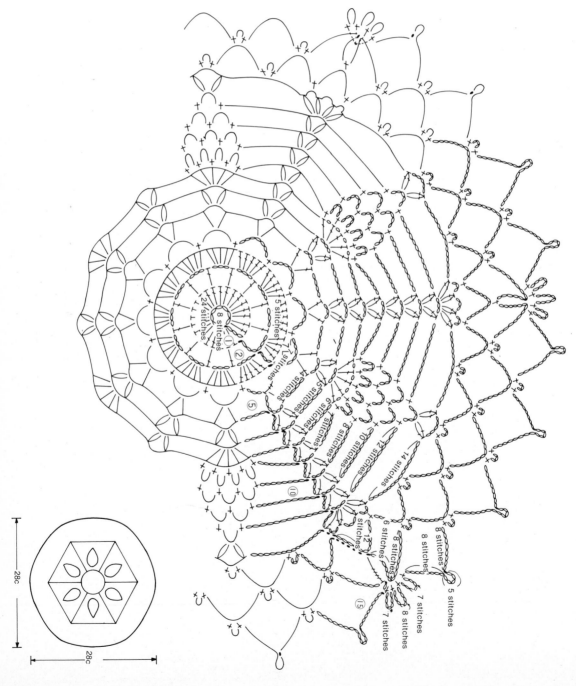

★**Materials:** Crochet cotton DMC (Soft twisted), 100 g white
(BLANC) Crochet hook size 1.75 mm
★**Finished size:** 37 cm × 78 cm
★**Instructions:** Chain 166. **Row 1:** start with 3 ch, 3 dc,

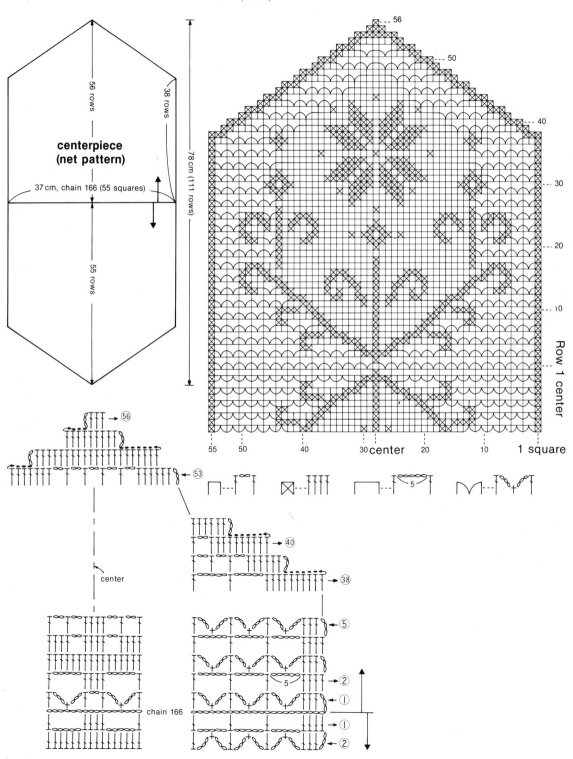

**centerpiece
(net pattern)**

56 rows

38 rows

78 cm (111 rows)

37 cm, chain 166 (55 squares)

55 rows

center

chain 166

33

Elegant Runners

That guarantee a run of good looks in any room you choose to use them

(33) Size: 37 cm × 78 cm. Instructions on page 53

(34) Size: 76 cm × 40 cm. Instructions on page 56

34

34

★**Materials:** Crochet cotton DMC (Soft twisted), 120 g white (BLANC) Crochet hook size 1.75 mm

★**Finished size:** 76 cm × 40 cm

★**Instructions: Row1:** chain 3 in ring, work with dc and ch sts, work 4 corners of diagonals similarly. **Rows 2—12:** work net pattern, being careful of the differrent patterns. Join 2nd motif to the next motif from Row 12, again being careful of different patterns. Border: **Row 1:** work sc around. **Row 2:** work net pattern. **Row 3:** work pattern with picots around.

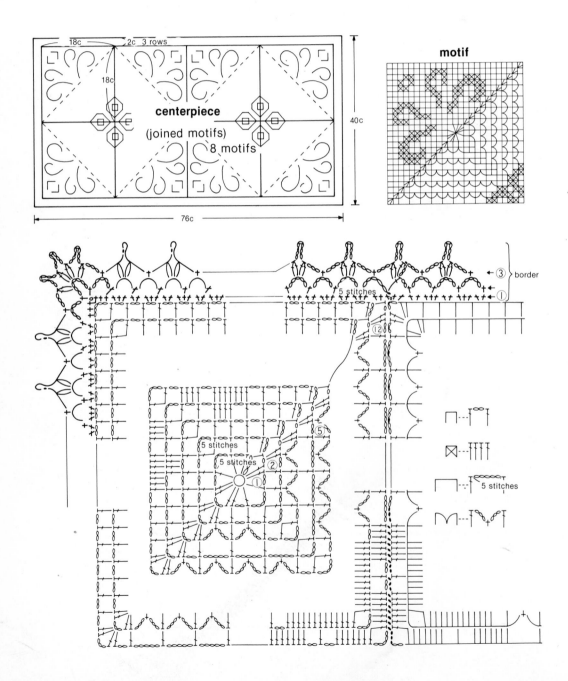

motif

18c   2c 3 rows

18c

centerpiece

(joined motifs)

8 motifs

40c

76c

border

5 stitches

5 stitches

5 stitches

5 stitches

35

Coaster on page 58

★**Materials:** Crochet cotton DMC (Soft twisted), 15 g saffron (727) Crochet hook size 1.75 mm
★**Finished size:** 13 cm × 12 cm
★**Instructions:** Chain 5 and close into a ring. **Row 1:** start with 1 ch, 12 sc, in ring. **Row 2:** start with 3 ch, °2 ch, 2 dc°, repeat. **Rows 3—6:** work 6 sets of pattern, increasing dc sts. **Rows 7—10:** work new pattern between patterns, decreasing dc sts. **Row 11:** work 6 patterns around, decorating with picots (3 ch).

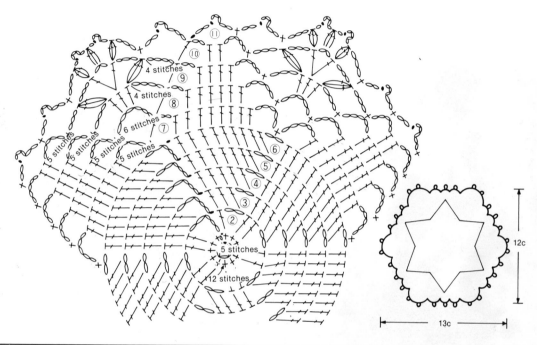

Design for Coaster 36 (shown on page 58).

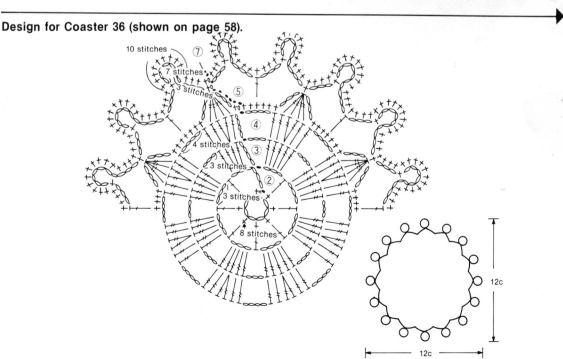

Assured Good Taste—

When these delightful coasters and placemats grace your dining table.

(35) Size: 13 cm × 12 cm. Instructions on page 57
(36) Size: 12 cm in diameter. Instructions on page 60
(37) Size: 12 cm in diameter. Instructions on page 60
(38) Size: 38 cm × 29 cm. Instructions on page 61

38

37

★**Materials:** Crochet cotton DMC (twisted), 15 g sky blue (518) Crochet hook size 1.75 mm

★**Finished size:** 12 cm in diameter

★**Instructions:** Chain 5 and close into a ring. **Row 1:** start with 5 ch, °2ch, 1 p (3 ch), 4 ch, 1 p (3 ch), 2 ch, 1 dbl tr°, repeat. **Row 2:** start with 1 ch, °1 sc, 7 ch°, repeat. **Row 3:** start with 4 ch, 2 ch, 2 tr, °1 sc, 3 ch, 1 sc, 2 tr, 2 ch, 2 tr°. repeat from ° to °. **Row 4:** start with 1 ch, ° 1 sc, 3 ch, 1 sc, 4 ch, 1 p, 7 ch, 1 p, 4 ch°, repeat from ° to °

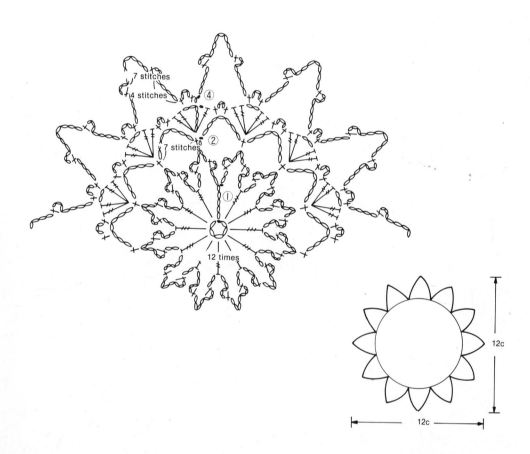

7 stitches
4 stitches
④
7 stitches
②
①
12 times

12c

12c

36

★**Materials:** Crochet cotton DMC (Soft twisted), 15 g peony rose (957), Crochet hook size 1.75 mm

★**Finished size:** 12 cm in diameter

★**Instructions:** Chain 7 and close into a ring. **Row 1:** start with 1 ch, 8 sc in ring. **Row 2:** start with 3 ch, °3 ch, 1 dc°, repeat. **Row 3:** start with 4 ch, 4 tr, °3 ch, 5 tr°, repeat from ° to °. **Row 4:** work by increasing ch and tr sts. **Row 5:** start with 1 ch, 1 sc, °3 ch, 1 cluster (4 tr), 3 ch, 7 sc°, repeat from ° to °. **Rows 6—7:** start with 1 ch, °° 1 sc, °3 ch, 1 sc-p (7 ch), 3 ch°, repeat from ° to ° twice, 1 dc°°, repeat from °° to °°. work last row with sc around.

38

Placemat on page 59

★**Materials:** Crochet cotton DMC (Soft twisted), 100 g white (BLANC) Crochet hook size 1.75 mm
★**Finished size:** 38 cm × 29 cm
★**Instructions:** Chain 10 and close into a ring. **Row 1:** start with 1 ch, 20 sc in ring. **Row 2:** start with 1 ch, °1 sc, 9 ch°, repeat. **Row 3:** start with 1 ch, 1 sc, °1 sc, 1 hdc, 11

dc, 1 hdc, 1 sc°, repeat from ° to °. **Rows 4—6:** work net pattern of 5 ch, make 4 9-ch corners on Row 6. **Row 7:** work net pattern and dc, join 2nd motif from Row 7. Join 12 motifs all together. **Border:** attach yarn at point indicated, start with 3 ch, °5 ch, 2 dc°, repeat from ° to ° around, work 2 rows.

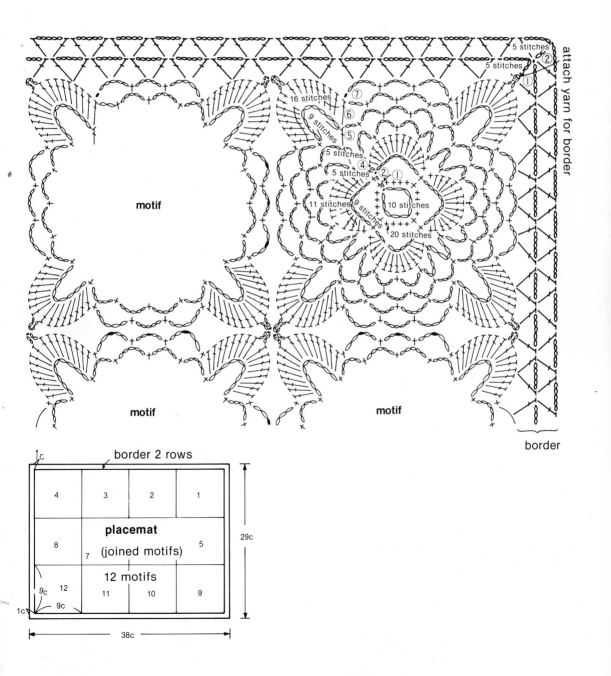

Beautiful Accents

Designs to make for the home scene, or for gorgeous gifts

(39) Size: 42 cm in diameter. Instructions on page 77

(40) Size: 42 cm × 42 cm. Instructions on page 80

★**Materials:** Crochet cotton DMC (Soft twisted), 30 g white (BLANC) Crochet hook size 1.50 mm

★**Finished size:** 25.5 cm × 22 cm

★**Instructions:** Chain 103. **Row 1:** start with 3 ch, 2 ch, 1 dc in 9th ch from hook, °2 ch, 1 dc°, repeat from ° to °

Rows 2—6: start with 3 ch, °2 ch, 1 dc°, repeat. **Rows 7—25:** follow design, working with dc. **Rows 26—31:** start with 3 ch, °2 ch 1 dc°, repeat. **Border:** attach yarn to first corner. Being careful to pick up all stitches, dc around. See design for corners.

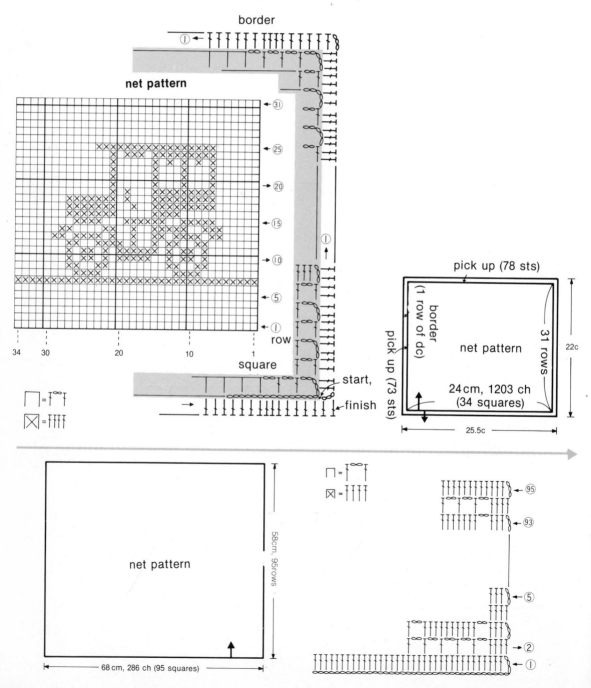

★**Materials:** Crochet cotton DMC (Soft twisted),200 g white (BLANC) Crochet hook size 1.50 mm

★**Finished size:** 68 cm × 58 cm

★**Instructions:** Chain 286. **Row 1:** work 1 dc in each st of foundation chain. **Row 2:** 4 dc on both ends, making 93 squares. **Rows 3—95:** work with dc and ch sts, following design carefully. Make sure all stitches are uniform because uneven stitches stand out in net patterns. You can alter the mood of the piece by changing the color on which it is mounted.

net pattern

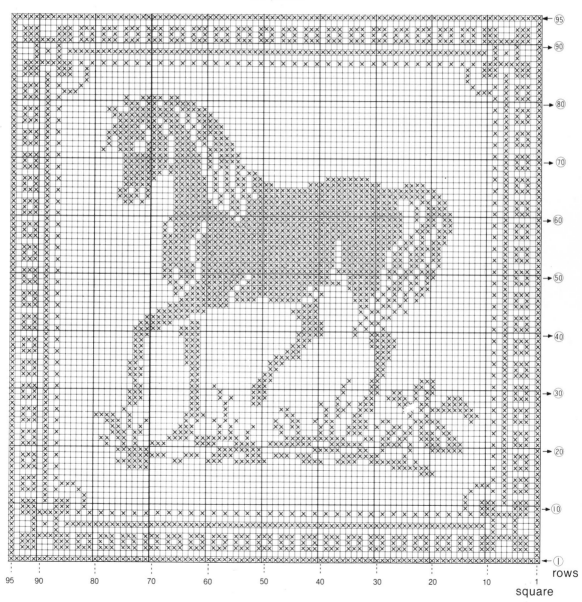

rows

square

Hang It!

A nostalgic treasure to frame for your home or for a very personalized gift.

(42) Size: 68cm×58cm. Instructions on page 65

★**Materials:** Crochet cotton DMC (Soft twisted), 30 g white (BLANC) Crochet hook size 1.50 mm
★**Finished size:** 29 cm in diameter
★**Instructions:** Chain 10 and close into a ring. **Row 1:** start with 1 ch, 16 sc in ring. **Row 2:** start with 4 ch, °2 ch, 1 tr°, repeat. **Rows 3—5:** work net pattern of 5 ch. **Row 6:** in loop of 5 ch of previous row, work °5 dc, 3 ch, 5 dc, 1 sc°, repeat. **Row 7:** start with 3 ch, 1 cluster (2 dc) °°3 ch, 1 cluster (3 dc), 5 ch, 1 sc, °5 ch, 1 sc°, repeat from ° to ° 6 times, 1 sc, 5 ch, 1 cluster (3 dc)°°, repeat from °° to °°.
Rows 8—14: complete 8 sets of pineapple patterns, start new fan shape pattern between the pineapple patterns.
Rows 15—17: continue fan-shape pattern, work picots (3 ch) around on last row.

★**Materials:** Crochet cotton DMC (Soft twisted) 35 g off-white (BLANC) Crochet hook size 1.50 mm

★**Finished size:** 33 cm in diameter

★**Instructions:** Chain 10 and close into a ring. **Row 1:** start with 3 ch, 23 dc, in ring. **Rows 2:** start with 3 ch, °3 ch, 1 dc°, repeat. **Row 3:** start with 3 ch, 3 ch, 1 dc, ° 2 ch, 1 dc, 3 ch, 1 dc, repeat from ° to °. **Rows 4—11:** work 12 shell patterns, make foundation for pineapple patterns, complete each pineapple pattern individually in 8 rows. Continue yarn from last pineapple patern, work sc and ch sts around. **Rows 2—4:** work net pattern. **Row 5:** finish with sc, hdc, dc sts.

★**Materials:** Crochet cotton DMC (Soft twisted), 20 g white (BLANC) Crochet hook size 1.75 mm

★**Finished size:** 25 cm in diameter

★**Instructions:** Chain 8 and close into a ring. **Row 1:** start with 3 ch, 23 dc in ring. **Row 2:** start with 3 ch, °2 ch, 1 dc°, repeat. **Row 3:** start with 3 ch, 1 ch, 1 dc, °3 ch, 1 dc, 1 ch, 1 dc°, repeat from ° to °. **Rows 4—6:** work by increasing number of ch and dc sts. **Row 7:** start with 3 ch, 1 dc, 3 ch, 2 dc, °3 ch, 1 sc, 3 ch, 2 dc, 3 ch, 2 dc°, repeat from ° to °. **Rows 8—14:** work 12 sets of pineapple patterns. **Row 15:** °1 sc, 5 ch, 5 dc, 1 ch, 1 p, 2 hc, 5 dc, 5 ch°, repeat.

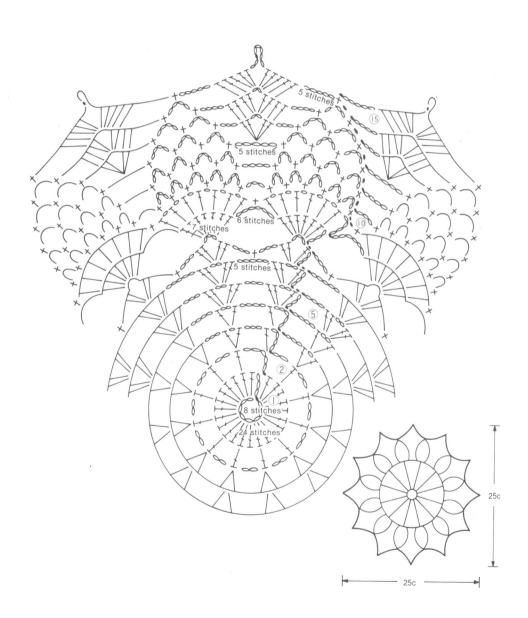

★**Materials:** Crochet cotton DMC (Soft twisted), 30 g white (BLANC) Crochet hook size 1.75 mm

★**Finished size:** 34 cm in diameter

★**Instructions:** Chain 7 and close into a ring. **Row 1:** start with 1 ch, 12 sc in ring. **Row 2:** start with 1 ch, °1 sc, 3 ch°, repeat. **Row 3:** start with 3 ch, 1 cluster (2 dc), °5 ch, 1 cluster (3 dc)°, repeat from ° to °. **Row 4:** start with 1 ch, °1 sc, 6 ch°, repeat. **Row 5:** 6 dc in loop of 6 ch of previous row. **Row 6:** start with 3 ch, 1 dc, °1 ch, 1 cluster (2 dc), 3 ch, 1 sc, 3 ch, 1 cluster (2 dc)°, repeat from ° to °. **Rows 7—14:** work 12 pattern sets. **Rows 15—19:** increase ch sts, work net pattern. **Row 20:** 6 dc in loop of 7 ch of previous row. **Row 21:** same as Row 6, except add picots around.

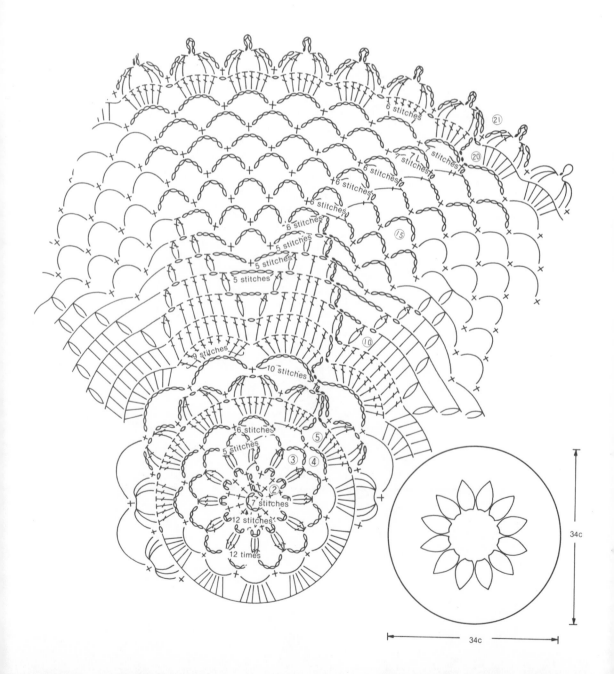

5

★**Materials:** Crochet cotton DMC (Soft twisted), 30 g white (BLANC) Crochet hook size 1.75 mm

★**Finished size:** 39 cm in diameter

★**Instructions:** Chain 10 and close into a ring. **Row 1:** start with 3 ch, 23 dc in ring. **Row 2:** start with 3 ch, 1 dc, °3 ch, 1 cluster (2 dc) °, repeat from ° to °. **Row 3:** start with 3 ch, 59 dc. **Row 4:** start with 3 ch, °3 ch, 4 dc°, repeat. **Row 5:** 9 dc in loop of 3 ch of previous row. **Rows 6—10:** work with ch and dc sts. **Row 11:** work sc around. **Rows 12—19:** work net and "V" patterns. **Row 20:** picots on top of each pattern.

★**Materials:** Crochet cotton DMC 30 g sevres blue (799)
Crochet hook size 1.50 mm

★**Finished size:** 28 cm in diameter

★**Instructions:** Chain 8 and close into a ring. **Row 1:** start
with 3 ch, 15 dc in ring. **Row 2:** start with 4 ch, 1 cluster
(2 tr), °7 ch, 1 cluster (3 tr)°, repeat from ° to °. **Row 3:** start
with 3 ch, 1 cluster (3 dc), °5 ch, 1 cluster (4 dc)°, repeat
from ° to °. **Row 4:** work sc around. **Row 5:** sc on cord
(same yarn as the doily), twisting at the same time. **Rows
6—13:** work net pattern. **Row 14:** work sc around. **Row
15:** same as Row 5, sc on cord.

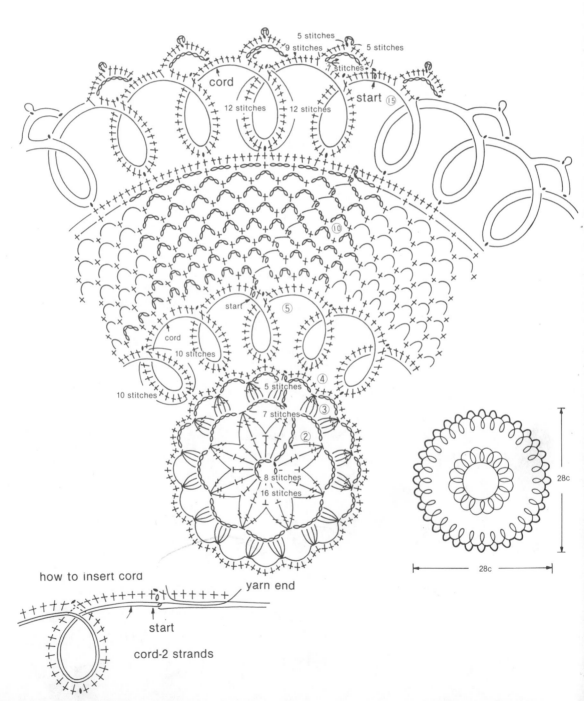

cord

5 stitches
9 stitches 5 stitches
7 stitches
12 stitches 12 stitches start ⑮

⑩

start ⑤

cord
10 stitches

10 stitches

5 stitches ④

7 stitches ③

②

8 stitches

16 stitches

28c

28c

how to insert cord

yarn end

start

cord-2 strands

★**Materials:** Crochet cotton DMC (Soft twisted), 35 g cream (746) Crochet hook size 1.50 mm

★**Finished size:** 28 cm in diameter

★**Instructions:** Row 1: 24 sc in ring. Row 2: start with 3 ch, dc in each sc of previous row. Row 3: start with 3 ch, 1 cluster (3 dc), °7 ch, 1 cluster (4 dc)°, repeat from ° to °. Row 4: work sc around. Rows 5—10: work net pattern, increasing number of ch sts. Row 11: work sc around. Rows 12—13: insert cord as in Doily 6. Flower motif: Row 1: start with 3 ch in ring, °2 ch, 1 dc°, repeat. Row 2: start with 1 ch, °1 sc, 3 ch, 1 cluster (3 dc), 3 ch°, repeat. Join to adjoining motif from 2nd motif from this row. Border: Rows 1—2: work ch and sc sts around. Row 3: same method as Row 12.

8

★**Materials:** Crochet cotton DMC (Soft twisted), 30 white (BLANC) Crochet hook size 1.75 mm

★**Finished size:** 31 cm in diameter

★**Instructions:** Chain 10 and close into a ring. **Row 1:** start with 3 ch, 31 dc in ring. **Rows 2—3:** net pattern around. **Row 4:** start with 3 ch, 4 dc, °2 ch, 1 dc, 2 ch, 5 dc°, repeat from ° to °. **Rows 5—7:** work 8 pattern sets. **Rows 8—18:** work patterns, using same method, work net pattern between patterns. **Row 19:** work pattern on top of each pattern (8 places), also work loops of dc and ch sts on top of net pattern.

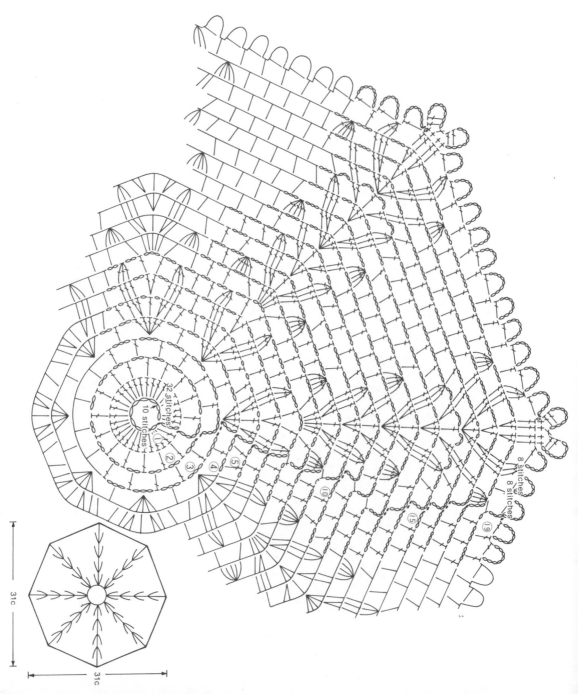

74

★**Materials:** Crochet cotton DMC (Soft twisted), 12 g (BLANC) Crochet hook size 1.75 mm

★**Finished size:** 22 cm in diameter

★**Instructions:** Chain 6 and close into a ring. **Row 1:** start with 3 ch, °2 ch, 1 dc°, repeat. **Row 2:** start with 4 ch, 47 tr. **Row 3:** start with 3 ch, °2 ch, 1 dc°, repeat. **Rows 4—5:** same as Row 3, increasing number of ch sts. **Row 6:** work 6 ch, 1 sc around. **Rows 7—12:** work 12 sets of pattern, work net pattern between patterns. **Row 14:** work sc around, making picots (3 ch) on top of each pattern.

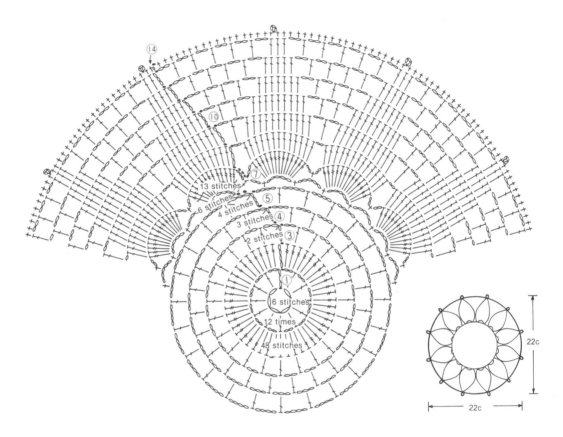

Design for Doily 14 (shown on page 30)

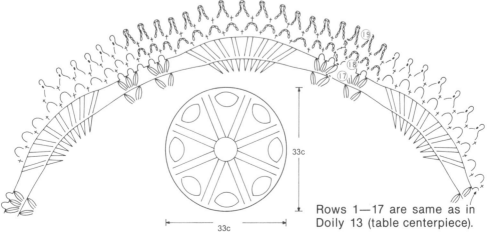

Rows 1—17 are same as in Doily 13 (table centerpiece).

★**Materials:** Crochet cotton DMC (Soft twisted), 12 g white (BLANC) Crochet hook size 1.75 mm

★**Finished size:** 23 cm in diameter

★**Instructions:** Chain 8 and close into a ring. **Row 1:** start with 3 ch, °2 ch, 1 dc°, repeat. **Row 2:** start with 3 ch, 3 dc, °3 ch, 4 dc°, repeat from ° to °. **Rows 3—7:** same method as Row 2 (be cafeful of number of ch and dc sts). **Row 8:** work net pattern of 5 ch. **Rows 9—14:** work 8 sets of fan patterns, work different pattern between fan patterns with sc. **Row 15:** start with 3 ch, 1 cluster (2 dc), °1 p (3 ch), 3 ch, 1 cluster (3 dc)°, repeat from ° to °, making picots on top of sc patterns as well.

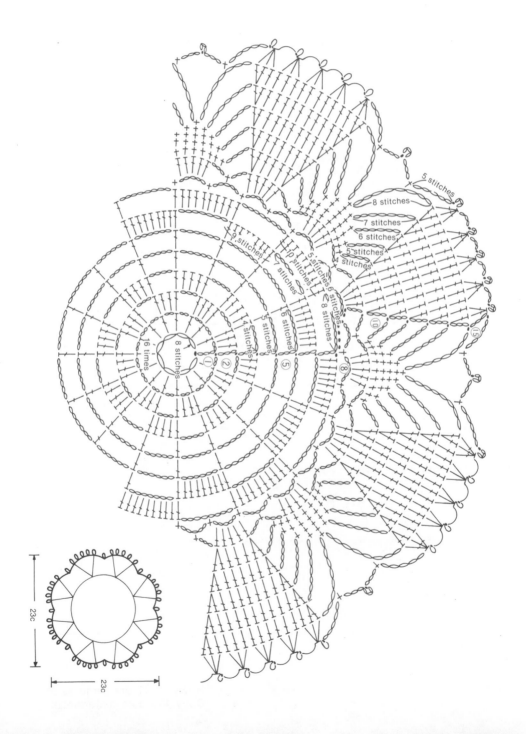

★**Materials:** Crochet cotton DMC (Soft twisted), 10 g sky blue (518) Crochet hook size 1.75 mm

★**Finished size:** 18 cm × 18 cm

★**Instructions: Row 1:** start with 3 ch in ring, °3 ch, 1 d°, repeat. **Row 2:** start with 3 ch, 1 dc, °2 ch, 1 cluster (2 dc), 1 ch, 1 p, 1 ch, 1 cluster (2 dc)°, repeat from ° to °. **Row**

3: start with 3 ch, 1 dc, 2 ch, 2 dc, °9 ch, 2 dc, 2 ch, 2 dc°, repeat from° to °. **Rows 4—8:** work 3 sets of fan and pineapple patterns. **Row 9:** start with 3 ch, 3 dc, °° (°7 ch, 1 sc°, repeat from ° to ° 9 times), 7 ch, 4 dc°°, repeat from °° to °°.

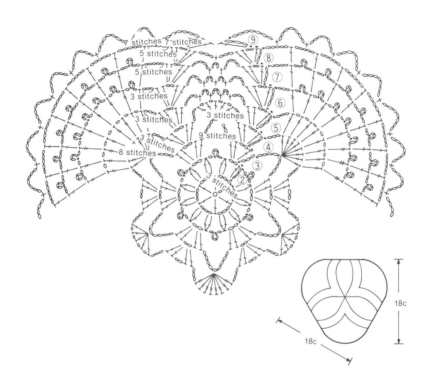

18c

18c

Doily No. 32

★**Materials:** Crochet cotton DMC (Soft twisted), 95 g white (BLANC) Crochet hook size 1.75 mm

★**Finished size:** 74 cm

★**Instructions:** Chain 8 and close into a ring. **Row 1:** start with 3 ch, 23 dc in ring. **Row 2:** start with 3 ch, °3 ch, 1

dc°, repeat. **Row 3:** 5 dc in loop of 3 ch of previous row. **Row 4:** work net pattern. **Rows 5—11:** work 6 sets of pattern. Join motifs at Row 11 with sl st starting with 2nd motif. Join pieces in 12 places. Finish 7 rows of border pattern. Design is shown on p. 78.

Doily No. 39

★**Materials:** Crochet cotton DMC (Soft twisted), 150 g (for 2 pillows) saffron (727) 2 42 cm-diameter foam cushions. Crochet hook size 1.75 mm

★**Finished size:** 42 cm in diameter

★**Instructions:** Chain 8 and close into a ring. **Row 1:** start with 3 ch, °1 ch, 1 dc°, repeat. **Row 2:** start with 1 ch, °1

sc, 3 ch°, repeat. **Row 3—4:** same as Row 2, increasing number of ch sts. **Rows 5—7:** work net pattern. **Row 8:** work 8 foundations for pineapple patterns. **Rows 9—38:** complete pineapple patterns. Design is shown on p. 79.

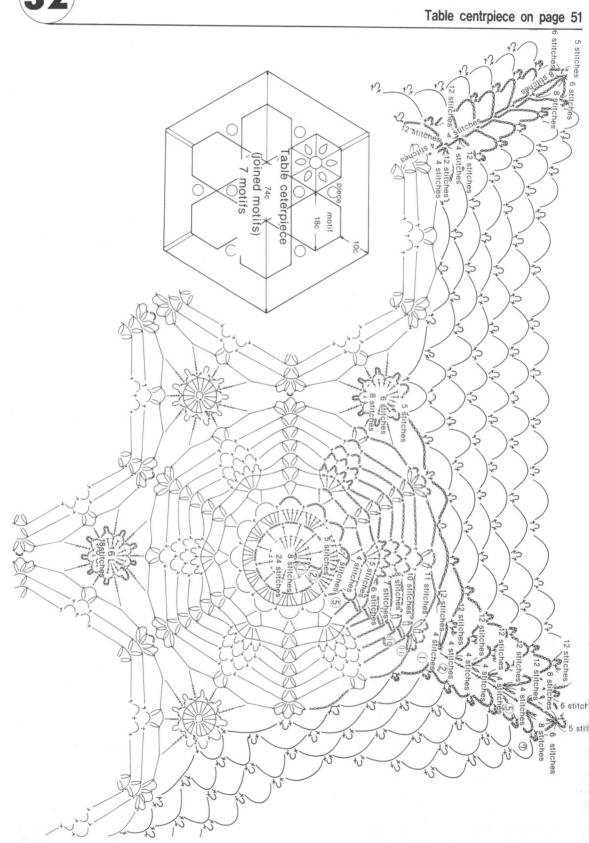

Table ceterpiece
(joined motifs)
7 motifs

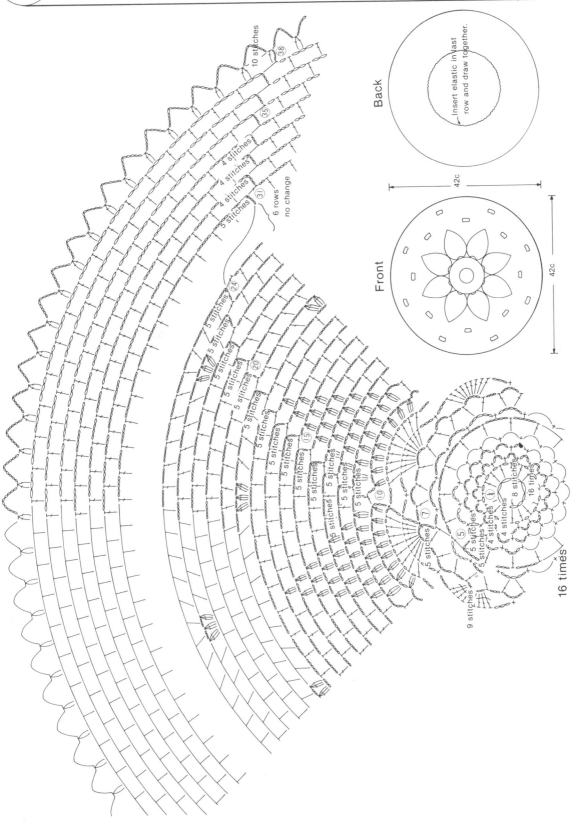

Back

Insert elastic in last row and draw together.

42c

Front

42c

10 stitches

38

35

4 stitches

4 stitches

4 stitches

5 stitches

31

6 rows no change

24

5 stitches

5 stitches

5 stitches

20

5 stitches

5 stitches

5 stitches

5 stitches

15

5 stitches

5 stitches

5 stitches

5 stitches

5 stitches

5 stitches

5 stitches

10

5 stitches

5 stitches

7

5 stitches

5 stitches

5

5 stitches

5 stitches

4 stitches

4 stitches

1

8 stitches

16 times

9 stitches

16 times

★**Materials:** Crochet cotton (Soft twisted), 220 g (for 2 pillows) white (BLANC) 2 42 cm-square foam cushions Crochet hook size 1.75 mm

★**Finished size:** 42 cm × 42 cm

★**Instructions: Front:** chain 163. **Row 1:** start with 3 ch, °2 ch, 1 dc°, repeat to make 54 squares. **Rows 2—5:** same as Row 1, work 54 squares. **Rows 6—49:** following design, work patterns. **Rows 50—54:** work net pattern. **Back:** foundation is same as front piece; work 54 rows of net pattern. With wrong side together. join three edges of front and back with 1 row of sc. Stuff pillows with foam and join remaining edge with sc.

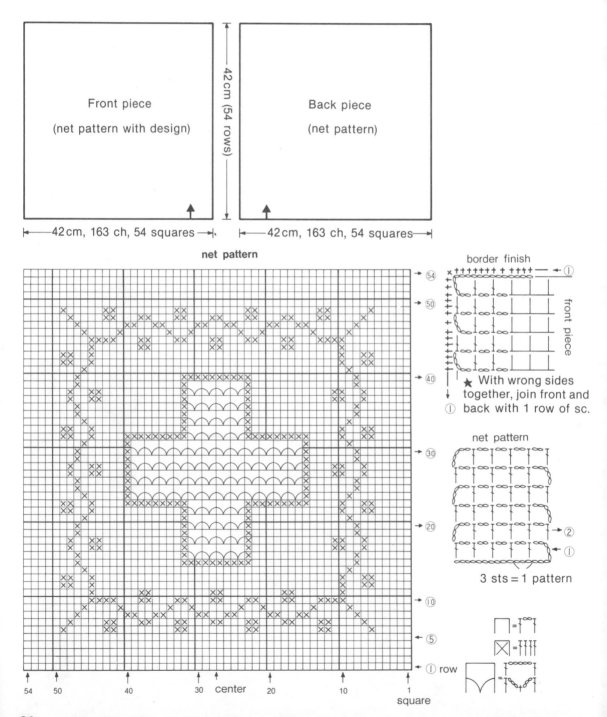

Front piece

(net pattern with design)

Back piece

(net pattern)

42 cm (54 rows)

|←——42 cm, 163 ch, 54 squares——→| |←——42 cm, 163 ch, 54 squares——→|

net pattern

border finish

front piece

★ With wrong sides together, join front and ① back with 1 row of sc.

net pattern

3 sts = 1 pattern

54   50   40   30 center 20   10   1

square

★ Joining with slip stitch

Work to postion of sl st, insert hook in loop to be joined from above , yarn over hook, draw yarn through loops on hook.

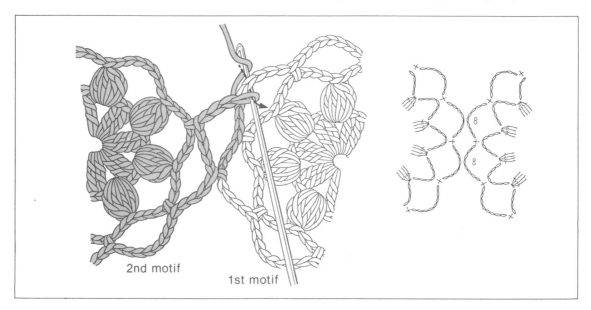

2nd motif

1st motif

★ Joining with single crochet

1. Work to position, insert hook in loop to be joined from below, single crochet.

2. Work remaining chain stitches.
3. Completed.

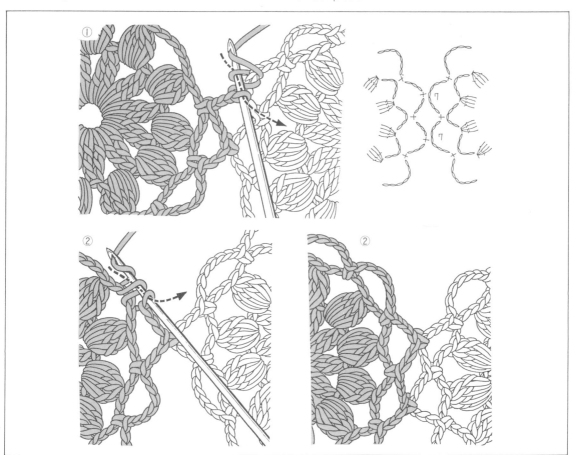

★ Before finishing
1. Fasten off yarn.
2. Check for stains.

★ Finished size
The size shown in this book is the size after ironing. Therefore, your piece of work will be slightly smaller than the ironed finished size.

★ Drawing guide lines
1. Draw circles and inner circles, according to the measurement of the pattern.
2. Draw division lines according to the number of patterns that make up the work. Do the same for straight crochet work.

★ Equipment used for finishing
1. Ironing board (containing springs so that stitches are not compressed.)
2. Iron
3. Towel
4. Pressing cloth (3 & 4 should be white cotton cloth)
5. Detergent (mild)
6. Spray starch
7. Spray
8. Pins
9. Finishing mount (brown craft paper)

★ How to pin
1. With wrong side up, place work on mount, pin the center.
2. Matching the guide lines, stretch your work to pin.
3. Berfore ironing, remove the center pin.

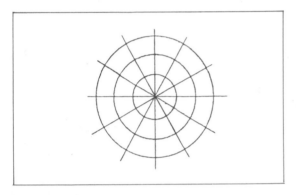

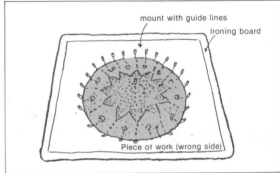

mount with guide lines
Ironing board
Piece of work (wrong side)

★ How to iron
1. Spray with spray starch
2. Apply hot iron to pressing cloth and press. (Be careful not to burn.)
3. Remove pins when your piece of work is completely dry.

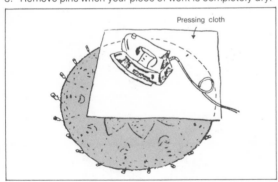

Pressing cloth

★ If soiled
Dissolve mild detergent in lukewarm water and squeeze or shake wash soiled piece in it gently. Rinse until water is clear. Wrap in towel to absorb water. Apply a little starch and finish as usual.

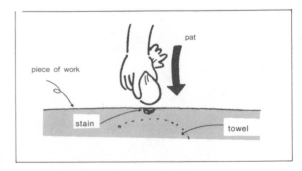

pat
piece of work
stain
towel

★ Stains
Stains come out better if you treat them immediately.
1. For small stains, place work on towel and pat with a detergent-soaked cloth. Change the position of the towel several times and pat repeatedly.

2. If the stain is not set too deep, it will come out in the wash. For stubborn stains, soak in water with a mild detergent (10 g per 1 liter). Depending on the type of stain, it should come out in 10 to 60 minutes. Finish as usual.

1100